RACE TO
VICTORY
LANE

Other books by Crystal Earnhardt:

Victory Lane

To order, call 1-800-765-6955.

Visit us at www.reviewandherald.com for information on other Review and Herald® products.

RACE TO
VICTORY
LANE

CRYSTAL EARNHARDT

REVIEW AND HERALD® PUBLISHING ASSOCIATION
Since 1861 | www.reviewandherald.com

The author assumes full responsibility for the accuracy of all facts
and quotations as cited in this book.

Texts credited to NIV are from the *Holy Bible, New International
Version*. Copyright © 1973, 1978, 1984, International Bible
Society. Used by permission of Zondervan Bible Publishers.

This book was
Edited by Jeannette R. Johnson
Cover designed by Pierce Creative
Interior designed by Freshcut Design
Cover photos: Man with flag: DigitalVision/PictureQuest
Electronic makeup by Shirley M. Bolivar
Typeset: Bembo 11/14

PRINTED IN U.S.A.

12 11 10 09   8 7 6 5

R&H Cataloging Service
Earnhardt, Crystal
    Race to victory lane.

        1. Earnhardt, John R.   I. Title.
                    [B]

ISBN 978-0-8280-1775-6

Dedicated

to the memory of

Dale Earnhardt

and to the little rascals of our family—

Carrie, Robby, Kelly,

Jesse, Cameron, and Kristina

CONTENTS

Introduction

Chapter 1   The Racetrack. 11

Chapter 2   The Decoy 15

Chapter 3   Car In Flames 23

Chapter 4   Time Stands Still 27

Chapter 5   Snookie. 30

Chapter 6   Angels on the Lookout 34

Chapter 7   Icy Waters. 38

Chapter 8   The Almost Murder. 44

Chapter 9   Buddy's Gang 49

Chapter 10   The License. 57

Chapter 11   A Tale of Death and Life 62

Chapter 12   John Meets Mr. Stubbs
             and the One-armed Man 67

Chapter 13   The Final Race 70

INTRODUCTION

This story begins during the 1950s, when the super speedway era of NASCAR was just beginning. Two young boys stood on the sidelines of a small backwoods racetrack in the little town of Gold Hill, North Carolina. Together, they watched the micro-midget cars zoom past.

The boys had much in common. They were just one year apart in age, and both had blue eyes and brown hair. Their fathers were entranced with speed and the thrill of flying past the checkered flag before all the other racers. And both boys were so excited they could practically spit dust.

They could not have known then that one of them, Dale Earnhardt, would become known as "The Intimidator." He would be immortalized as a legend in NASCAR racing, savoring 76 wins in victory lane.

The other boy, John Earnhardt, though he would not become nearly as famous, would take a different road to glory. This road would not be paved with asphalt or filled with the sound of cheering fans. Nevertheless, it would lead to the ultimate Victory Lane.

This is his story.

—Crystal Earnhardt

CHAPTER I

THE RACETRACK

"John, you're not going to the racetrack until you finish your lunch," Mom said as she hurried from the kitchen. "Now get chewing!" Her voice trailed behind her down the hall as she made mental notes of all the tasks yet to be done. "I need to make sure the popcorn supply is ample and that the sodas are cold," she reminded herself.

John crammed a slice of bread into his mouth, and then drowned it with a swallow of milk. He had looked forward to this day for months. At last his dad's dream of opening a racetrack had come true.

For weeks he had listened to the distant hum of a bulldozer about a half mile away through the woods behind his house. Day after day it dug the red clay dirt and packed it into a solid track. Then came the roar of dump trucks hauling more loads of dirt. The hammers had nailed hundreds of boards together to form the bleachers, the popcorn stand, and the announcer's box. Then came the evenings of practice when Dad and the other racers revved their engines and drove round and round on the hard-packed dirt track.

The whole family, from Mom and his two sisters, Judy and Jean (whom everyone called Snookie), to his older brother, Jimmy, and his baby brother, Rondy, had stood in the bleachers during practice to cheer them on until their voices grew hoarse and flying dust choked them. Sweat trickled down their backs.

Eventually Judy, who hated to get dirty, took the baby to a spot under the trees where Rondy could play and breath clean air. To John, dust and heat were but minor discomforts. Nothing could compel him to take his eyes off the track until the winner sped past the checkered flag.

"We've got to do something about that dust," his dark-haired mother had told Dad after the track cleared. "The cars kick up so much that we can't even see you out there!"

"You think you've got it bad," Dad replied as he mopped his grimy face with his handkerchief. "There were times I couldn't even see the track! We'll wet it down about an hour before the race." He held out his once-white handkerchief for her to see. It was the color of red clay.

At the memory of his father's words, John dropped the glass of milk, grabbed his cap, slammed the screen door behind him, and raced toward the track. If he hurried, he might be there before the water truck arrived.

Even though it would be an hour before the race began, cars full of people were already in line to park. He heard several familiar voices calling to him as he ran past.

"Hey, boy, where's the fire?" one old man with a white beard yelled from a black pickup truck.

John waved and kept running. He was gasping for breath by the time he reached the bleachers. And not a moment too soon! An old, creaky truck, with a rusty 300-gallon tank on its back, had just lumbered onto the track and stopped. A man jumped from the cab and attached a long pipe to the back of the truck. The pipe, with holes punched along its length, hung suspended about six inches from the ground. After a few minutes he climbed back into the truck and started driving slowly around the track. Water poured from the holes and doused the dirt. The track immediately looked darker.

John stood transfixed by the whole scene before him: the watering truck, the crowds of people climbing up the bleachers for seats, the small cars with their loud motors, the smell of damp earth and gasoline. It was *big;* bigger than he had imagined. So big, in fact, that the local rescue squad truck was parked on the sidelines, in case of emergencies, and some of their men were selling tickets. "Rowan County Rescue Squad" was embroidered on their caps and shirts, so it was easy to identify them.

And to think that it was all because of his dad! Somehow the thought of it made him feel a little bigger, a little more important.

John decided to run over to where his dad stood, surrounded by a group of men. *Maybe some of them were really important people like the mayor, or the sheriff,* he thought.

"Good to see you, Ralph," he heard his dad saying to a man who had a boy about John's age leaning against him. "Been doing a lot of big-time racing lately? Heard you did good in Hickory."

"Yep. It beats running from the law!"

The two men laughed. John wondered what he meant by running from the law, but decided that now wasn't a good time to ask.

"Your boy must be about my son's age," Dad commented.

"Yes, sir," the man responded. "This is my son Dale."

Dad looked thoughtful for a moment and then turned toward his curious son. "John, I want you to meet Dale Earnhardt. You boys share the same last name. And your ancestors"—he paused and laughed—"had a lot more in common than just a family tree!"

John wondered if Ralph's little joke about running from the law and dad's comment about his and Dale's ancestors sharing something were connected to each other. It seemed that most of the drivers shared a common bond, or brotherhood, of some kind. He just didn't know what.

THE DECOY

As the weeks went by John and the other boys, whose fathers competed at the track, began to look forward to Sundays. Although none of the boys knew it, their destinies were being shaped around that track. Two brothers, Billy and Bobby Myers, often came to race their micro-midgets. The young Myers boy who came with them would one day be the popular "Chocolate Myers," who would be employed by "The Intimidator" to furnish the gas for his car at the NASCAR races.

Who could have guessed that two of the boys who played tag and other games together would one day be famous in NASCAR history? At the moment they were hiding in the bushes so they could hear firsthand the stories the men told each other—not the later tamed-down version reserved for the women and children.

The men were discussing the final Grand National race that was to be held on Daytona Beach. Up to this time racing events were held on the open beach, but because of large numbers of people who attended and the wear and tear on the beach itself, they were forced to build a track farther inland.

About 35,000 people turned out for the farewell

Beach-Road event. Two men, Turner and Goldsmith, were locked in a ferocious duel for the win when Turner spun out into the ocean, allowing Goldsmith a 10-second lead. But the ending caught everyone off guard as Goldsmith, who had lost the use of his windshield wipers, sped past the north turn on the final lap and drove on up the beach.

Some of the men laughed at how surprised Goldsmith must have felt when he discovered that he was driving up the beach alone until the storyteller, a wiry man with nails as black as grease, described how the undaunted Indianapolis 500 veteran realized his mistake and quickly cut a 180-degree turn. He then proceeded to not only catch back up but to cross the finish line a few feet ahead of the speeding Turner.

By now everyone, including the boys hiding in the bushes, were laughing and slapping their knees in admiration. That's how races were—surprise ending after surprise ending. Some racers lost, no matter how hard they tried. Others won through sheer determination, skill, and a stroke of good fortune.

As the boys ran off to more important pursuits, they had no idea how their futures would be so intertwined with each other. But they did know that Sundays around the racetrack always proved to be exciting. There were footraces for the kids, and sometimes the kids even got to race in a real micro-midget car on the track!

Besides the races that took place on Sunday afternoons, John had another reason for loving that day. The law required that on Sundays The Grill, a small restaurant and bar that his mom and dad owned and operated beside the house, had to be closed. Nor could beer or alcoholic beverages be sold on the day that most people in the community understood to be "holy."

Sometimes John's mom insisted that they all go to Sunday school. But lately, she and Dad were suffering so badly from a hangover that they didn't get up in time. While they slept it off, John and his sister, Snookie, would get in their own micro-midgets and race around The Grill parking lot or practice leg races on the track.

But on this Sunday neither of them felt like racing or playing games of any kind. The night before, something scary had happened. It was so bad that John had to get away to sort things out. He grabbed his fishing pole and headed down to Greer's pond.

Greer's pond was the local hangout for the neighborhood boys. It was nothing more than a large pond in the middle of a field with just enough trees for shade, just enough blackberry bushes to provide a healthful snack during the summer, and just enough fish to make it a challenge.

To get to it John had to walk down the road and through a large patch of woods. The walk was quiet and peaceful, and ordinarily John would have been more aware of the birds flitting among the trees, or the rabbits that stood perfectly still until he came within a foot of them. But his thoughts were so preoccupied with the events of last night that he could think of little else. Perhaps the serenity of nature would calm his still shaking hands. He stood on the bank, baited his hook, and slung it in. Once the fishing line was in the water, John began reliving the previous night.

::::::

Problems had begun soon after Dad pulled the station wagon up to the basement door. Then he and Mom loaded boxes of alcoholic beverages to be delivered to a private party in the next county. The problem was that the next county was considered a "dry" county, which meant it was illegal to sell alcoholic beverages there. Dad knew that, but money and the thrill of outwitting the law enticed him. To complicate matters, a phone call before the scheduled trip warned him that the highway patrol was on the lookout. But Dad refused to back out of the deal.

"Once the boxes are loaded," he told Mom, "cover them with a blanket and pillows. Then you and the two youngest kids get yourselves ready."

"You mean we're all going?" Mom asked in disbelief.

"Sure. We'll put the kids under the blanket too. That way, if anybody stops us we'll just tell them not to disturb our sleeping kids. Judy and Jimmy are too big, but John and Snookie are still short enough to make good decoys. What officer would move a sleeping kid?"

John didn't like it one bit being described as short. Mom had always told him that boys grew taller when they became teenagers, but he still had a couple years to go. And having to "sleep" on the hard boxes only added injury to insult.

"Now, Johnny, you'll be getting paid for this job. Aren't you saving money for a new bike?" Mom tried to soothe things over by calling him by her pet name.

John squinted. He'd been saving up for a new bike for a long time. One that had high, silver handlebars; a long, blue, vinyl banana seat; a large, black, knobby back tire; and blue sparkle metallic paint. He had wanted it ever since he saw it parked outside the Carolina Tire Company. The promise of money made the bike seem a reality. He could almost see it parked in the garage beside Dad's micro-midget cars.

He sighed, thinking about the ride. What if the police caught them? A dread of what could happen overshadowed even the promise of a new bicycle. His parents might be put in jail. There might be bad things written about them in the newspaper, hurtful things that his friends' parents would read. Then they wouldn't let their children play with him.

And where would he and his brothers and sisters be if Mom and Dad were sent away? They couldn't live alone. He had heard horror stories of orphanages and foster homes. It seemed too big a burden to bear even thinking about what could happen. But there didn't seem to be any way out. He couldn't tell his father not to take such risks. So he remained quiet, and when the sky turned to shades of black, he and Snookie climbed in on the makeshift bed in the back of the station wagon.

The illegal goods were soon safely delivered. Dad went inside to collect his money and have a quick drink with the boys. "Just to be sociable," he winked at Mom.

After waiting in the car for about 45 minutes, Mom went inside to see what had happened to him. The hours slowly ticked by. At first John and Snookie amused themselves by watching men and women going in and out of the party. Most of them went in dressed very well in suits and ties, but when they came out their shirts were open at the neck and their ties were all crooked. Some were laughing loudly and acting foolishly. They staggered and bumped into each other. At first it was funny, but after a couple hours it wasn't funny anymore. It was sickening.

The music floated out the windows and through the doors every time they opened. It was too dark to play "I spy" or any other games. So they told stories to each other until neither one of them could think of another story. Every time the door opened they would strain their eyes in the dark, hoping to make out the familiar shape of their parents. Eventually, Snookie leaned her head against the window and fell asleep. With nothing to do, John closed his eyes and dreamed of the shiny blue bike that he hoped to buy soon.

It was after midnight when Mom and Dad stumbled out to the car. At first, Dad couldn't find his car keys, and Mom's speech was slurred.

"They're stone drunk," Snookie whispered to John. "Do you think they can drive?"

They soon found out. When Dad almost backed into another car, Mom cursed at him and then slumped over.

John and Snookie moved up to the back of the front seat. About five miles down the road, Dad's head began to nod and the car veered into the left lane. Snookie screamed and Dad jerked the steering wheel. Fortunately, since it was so late at night there was no traffic on the roads. The next time Dad began nodding, John stood up and leaned over Dad's head and took the wheel.

"Crawl into the front seat," John told his sister, "and work the gas pedal and the brakes."

"But how can I?" Snookie sobbed in fright.

"Just do it! Get Dad's foot off the gas. You're small enough to sit between him and the steering wheel."

Snookie nodded resolutely and obeyed. John knew he could count on her. She was a tough girl and agile as a cat.

The car squealed to a stop as Snookie found the brakes. Then it lurched ahead when she found the gas pedal. She couldn't see that well and depended on John to give concise directions, which he wasn't used to doing. It was a wonder that their heads didn't snap off as the car stopped and started every few feet.

John had his hands full just trying to keep the car in the right lane. Steering a car over another person's head isn't easy. Fortunately, both kids had had experience driving the micro-midgets, and somehow their combined efforts got them home.

When at last they pulled into the driveway and stopped, Judy ran out to meet them. "I've been worried sick!" she cried. "What happened?"

"We had to drive home," John quietly told her.

Judy looked with disgust on her parents, who were both slumped over and out cold. "Well, come on in and get to bed. The sun will be up before too long."

"What about Mom and Dad?" Snookie asked.

"Leave them here. Serves them right."

: : : : : :

John snapped out of his thoughts when his cork disappeared under the water. He pulled the line in, but it was too late; the fish had slipped off the hook. He baited it again with a fat worm and tossed it back into the water. He'd have to pay more attention.

But not even a hungry fish could keep his thoughts from wandering back to his parents. Alcohol controlled their actions. Under its influence they had no thoughts for anyone but themselves. Dad's driving the previous night could have killed them all. It wasn't fair of his parents to put Snookie and himself in such danger.

Then he remembered something he'd heard at the racetrack about running from the law. Bootlegging seemed to be a "second job" for some racers. Was that what the men were joking about?

John could understand why some counties chose to make the sale of alcohol illegal. He had seen with his own eyes how the people at the party had acted last night after drinking it. He shuddered when he remembered how Dad had driven after drinking it.

One thing he knew for sure: alcohol would never be a temptation for him. He knew firsthand how those who drank it became slaves to a stupid bottle. He made up his mind that he would avoid it always.

CHAPTER 3

CAR IN FLAMES

"Good morning!" Judy smiled at Snookie and John as she glided through the kitchen on her tiptoes like a ballerina.

John looked up from his plate of white rice, eggs, and toast that Dad had cooked for breakfast. (Mom always slept late on Sundays.)

Judy leisurely poured herself a glass of orange juice and sipped it slowly with a dreamy look in her eyes.

"I wondered if you were going to get up before lunch," Dad said, peering over his morning paper. "But I figured the racetrack queen needed her beauty rest."

Startled, Judy looked at the clock. "Oh!" she cried out. "It's 9:00. I've got tons of things to do—fix my hair, get my dress ironed—"

John shook his head as Judy tore out of the kitchen quite the opposite from the way she had entered. Judy was the oldest and the most difficult to understand—not that John spent any time trying. She loved twirling the baton around like a drum majorette and looking at herself in the mirror. She took control of the whole house when Mom was working and bossed everybody else like they were her servants. As far as he was concerned she had either let the baton hit her head once too many times or he had an alien for a stepsister.

He guessed that her parents' divorce had been hard on Judy. The marriage had dissolved when she was just a little girl. Too young to understand the complications of a marriage gone sour, she had been old enough to miss her father, who went back to New York and was seldom heard from again.

Maybe in her childish mind, she felt as though she had done something wrong that made her daddy go away. Or maybe she just plain resented another man taking her daddy's place. Whatever the reason, Judy kept an invisible wall between herself and her stepfather until she was about 13 years old.

On Father's Day everyone else worked hard to make or buy a present for Dad. But not Judy. She stood around watching as he *oohed* and *aahed* at the handkerchiefs Snookie gave him and the socks that John had bought. Once Snookie asked her what she had gotten for Dad, but Judy only tossed her head defiantly and said, "He's not my father."

After that Dad went out of his way to do things for Judy. True, he wasn't a perfect father (he drank every other weekend), but he did provide them all with a comfortable house and plenty of food, clothes, and toys. And he never physically beat them.

His latest gesture of goodwill toward her was to pronounce her the racetrack queen. As the queen, Judy wore a tiara on her head and a fancy dress such as a girl would wear to a high school prom. After the announcer declared the winner, Judy would hand him a trophy and kiss him. John guessed it made her feel important, but he felt sorry for the winner, who had to stand there and smile through it.

The rest of the morning went by quickly as the whole family prepared for the afternoon race. John practiced running around the track. All the boys got to participate in a footrace, and he wondered who would win. Dale had longer legs, but was he a fast runner? He soon found out he was. John had never met anyone who wanted to win as badly as Dale Earnhardt. But Dale didn't gloat for long over the footrace because the micro-midget cars were already lining up.

The two boys stood as close to the track as safety permitted. "One day that's gonna be me out there, but my car will be like my dad's," Dale remarked.

John knew that Ralph, Dale's dad, competed each Saturday in NASCAR races.* Mom and Dad had taken him a number of times to Daytona Beach in Florida to watch them. It looked like fun, but . . .

"Gentlemen, start your engines!" the announcer's voice interrupted his thoughts.

All else was lost in a roar of motors starting, dust flying up his nose, and people shouting. Around and around the track the cars flew. First one would lead, another would pass, and then one would spin out. People ate popcorn and hot dogs, drank sodas, and smiled a lot.

And then it happened.

Number 25 decided to pass Dad on the inside of the track but got too close. Tire bumped tire as they approached the curve. Suddenly Dad's car was spin-ning out of control, right in the path of the rest of the drivers. Some veered off the track and into the infield to avoid hitting him. Others tried to judge the direction he was spinning and go around him, but it was too late. One car after another knocked him this way and that until one clipped him at the back and flipped his car into the air.

John watched in horror as the car's gas tank burst into flames and the vehicle landed with a thud upside down before rolling over several times. Smoke now mingled with dust in a thick haze. The rescue squad was on the track within minutes, though it seemed like an eternity to those who stood, frozen, in the bleachers.

He could see men running to the burning flames, trying to jerk Dad out. But Dad wasn't moving; the fire was too hot to linger. He vaguely heard a woman screaming, "He's gonna burn! He's burning alive!" It felt to John like waking up from a nightmare and not being able to breathe. Except this was real!

John began running toward the now-still form of his father, but he felt as if he was in slow motion. He heard a familiar voice as someone rushed past him, jarring him to his senses. It was Judy, sailing down the track like a deer in flight, skirts flying and crown forgotten. "That's my father!" she screamed. "That's my father!"

---

*In the beginning of NASCAR the races were on Saturday, not Sunday as they are now.

CHAPTER 4

Time Stands Still

The crowd held their breath as several men tried unsuccessfully to pull John's dad from the flaming inferno. Just when all seemed hopeless, a man was seen running down the track, swinging a machete. Within minutes the safety belts were slashed in two, and John's dad was carried to the waiting rescue vehicle. Sirens wailed as the ambulance rushed him away.

Everything had happened so fast. John and Snookie stared as their mom handed the baby to Pearlie, their closest neighbor, and fled to a waiting vehicle. She didn't need to explain. Everyone knew that she had to be with her husband.

As soon as the track was cleared, the race continued. The drivers seemed to be a lot less daring; the crowd less enthusiastic. Judy, forgetting that she was supposed to give the winner a trophy and a kiss, took the baby from Pearlie and herded the rest of the kids back to the house.

"We need to stay by the phone," she said quietly. "Mama will call."

John stared at her. Was this the same girl who, minutes before, had outrun and outscreamed him all the way to the track? How could she be so hysterical one minute and so totally calm the next? He didn't dare question her. Instinctively he knew that beneath her calm exterior lay a firebomb waiting to go off. Even baby Rondy lay still in her arms without a whimper. Together, they all walked home.

The house was quiet, so quiet that John could hear the clock ticking on the mantle. He heard the people cheering down at the track. Knowing that the race must be over, he went to the window and watched the cars file down the lane as they left the track.

He remembered a saying that his teacher had once quoted when he was late for class: "Time and tide wait for no man." She then explained that time and ocean tides don't stop for anything or anybody. But as John watched the clock, time seemed to be standing still. Would Mama never call?

After an eternity, Mom and Dad appeared. "He's fine," Mom assured them as she walked into the house. "A bit bruised; a few burns—but he is fine."

"What did the doctor do?" Judy asked.

"He regained consciousness before they reached the hospital," Mom explained. "They dunked his head in a bucket of water and gave him a shot of whiskey for pain.★

"Well, I never!" Judy began. "Dunked his head in a bucket! I'll bet he was too cheap to pay a doctor for a decent examination. Craziest thing I ever heard of."

James brushed off his children's concerns. He ruffled their hair, got a drink, and then meandered out to assess the damage to his car. Terrified that he might collapse at any minute, John followed him all the way to the track. He watched as his father stared at the heap of charred metal. "Somebody up there was watching over me today," his father muttered.

: : : : : :

The next week was busy as James and his neighbor, Bill, worked on the car. All the kids were so glad to have their father alive that they willingly offered to help. With combined effort they got it repaired in time for Sunday's race. The crowd cheered madly as James drove number 00 to the starting line. And that week he won! Judy proudly walked to the winner's circle. She gave James a hug and kiss as she handed the trophy to him.

Looking back, John realized that something major had happened to Judy and to his father the day of the accident. It wasn't something that could be measured with a stick or noticed by a stranger. It dealt with the heart. Somehow they had developed a new understanding and respect for each other. You might call it love between a daughter and her stepfather.

It was a great discovery.

---

*Whiskey used to be given as a pain reliever. There are much better alternatives!

CHAPTER 5

Snookie

While Judy was considered the queen of the racetrack, Jean was considered the daredevil of the whole town. Unlike Judy, whose hair was always in place and her clothes neat and tidy, Jean's long locks were pulled back in a ponytail and her pants were usually patched in several places where she had slid down a tree or gotten caught by a barbwire fence. Everyone called her by her nickname, "Snookie," which didn't exactly lend itself to any feminine airs.

John felt that he was about the unluckiest boy in the town to have two sisters with such different personalities. Judy bossed him around by giving him a new job every time he walked in the door, and Snookie outjumped him, outraced him, and then talked him into reckless adventures in which he always got caught. He didn't know which sister was worse.

Snookie's latest escapade began when Dad announced that he was going to compete in a micro-midget race in Ocala, Florida, and the whole family could go.

Aside from a few spats in the car over territory rights, the trip down south turned out to be fun. Everyone was in high spirits when the race began, and the skies were clear and sunny. But as with most races, it got pretty boring about halfway through. The initial excitement had worn off after watching the cars go around and around the track about 20 times.

Suddenly Snookie spied something shiny under the bleachers. She punched John in the arm while pointing excitedly below. "Look! I bet it's a ring, or some money. Let's take a look."

It seemed like a harmless idea, and the sun did feel awfully hot as they sat on the metal seats. "All right," John agreed. "Let's go!"

Within a few minutes Snookie found a shiny dime. Then John found one. "Let's see who can find the most!" Snookie yelled, trying to be heard over the roar of engines. The two scrambled in a mad dash to find treasure that had fallen out of people's pockets as they sat in the bleachers.

Exactly how it happened no one is sure, but it seemed that both of them spied the same shiny object at the same time. In her haste to get to it before John, Snookie tripped and fell down. Unfortunately, she landed on a board with a nail sticking straight up. She fell with such force that the nail went completely through her lip.

Snookie's cry could be heard even above the roar of the crowd. When Mom saw the blood spurting out of her mouth, she grabbed some towels from a soda stand and pressed them against the lip to stop the flow of blood. Then she rushed Snookie to the car and sped off to the hospital. Those who saw them going said Mom should have been in the race.

Of course, John received a good scolding that night. Everybody figured that he must have shoved

Snookie in the spirit of competition. After all, he was at the scene of the accident.

Then there was the time, when they were younger, that Snookie talked all of them—including Judy and Jimmy—into making mud pies with her after a spring rain. A drain ditch by the roadside proved to be the best spot. John played along at first, but just couldn't pretend for long that the small brown mud balls were chocolate cakes. They looked more like missiles to him.

When an 18-wheeler came past them, Snookie jumped up and threw a mud ball. It splattered neatly against the sides of the long trailer. "Don't do that," Judy warned her. But Snookie got a gleam in her eye, and the game was on.

All went well as long as the trucks kept coming. After a dry spell of long minutes with no 18-wheelers, John jumped up and aimed for a car. The driver had her window down, her elbow propped up on the open windowsill. John's mud pie hit her arm and splattered all over the side of her face.

The car's taillights came on. "She's stopping!" Snookie screamed.

All four kids jumped up and made a mad dash to the house. They opened the door and raced to the bedroom, where they dived under the bed.

Moments later the doorbell rang. They could hear a shrill voice speaking, and then Mom yelled, "Judy! Jimmy! Snookie! Johnny! Get in here!"

Reluctantly they crawled out and slowly made their way down the hall. The woman's face was red and angry—and mud-spattered. Nobody wanted to

Dale's father, Ralph, now followed the NASCAR events on a weekly basis. Many of the races were out of state, and he couldn't get back home in time for the local races. Dale lived in Kannapolis, which was just far enough away to put him in a different school.

When Ralph did visit the racetrack, he often told stories about racing that kept kids sitting on the edge of their seats. He told one in particular that John loved to hear again and again. It was about two men who had driven all day and all night to get to the race. When they finally arrived, they fell asleep on the grass while waiting for the chance to compete. They were so tired and still that no one knew they were there. When it was time for the race to begin, the cars lined up, and one drove right over them! They weren't killed, but they wound up speeding to a hospital in an ambulance instead of speeding past the checkered flag.

"Wow!" John exclaimed. "Nothing that exciting ever happens at our track."

"I don't call that exciting," Judy sniffed. "People getting bones crushed is not exciting."

"We can thank the Lord for that," Mom added. "Your dad's accident was all the excitement I can stand."

Somehow the mention of God set John to thinking. Mom had made him attend Vacation Bible School at the Methodist church that summer. The teacher had taken him aside repeatedly to tell him how much God loved him.

"See this picture?" the teacher said, holding up a scene of two children walking over a perilous bridge. "Their angels are walking right beside them."

"Yes, ma'am," John had answered.

"If you love God, your angels will walk beside you, too."

"Do the angels walk beside people who don't love Him?" John asked.

The teacher nodded. "Yes, angels are there. They can't always keep bad things from happening if we persist in disobeying God, but they are always doing their best to remind us that God loves us."

"I wonder if the angels were beside me driving the car when Dad passed out at the wheel," John muttered under his breath, recalling the nighttime bootlegging incident when his father had drunk too much alcohol.

The question stayed with him all week. Mom and Dad clearly weren't obeying God. Although he hadn't read much of the Bible that his grandmother had given him, he knew enough to realize that alcohol was bad. If it were bad, then it would be disobeying God to drink it. If that were the case, then were his parents bad? Would they not go to heaven because of alcohol? The thought troubled him.

Although he had absolutely no idea where to look, he opened his Bible each night and read a chapter. Some of the words didn't make any sense to him, but others made him feel warm inside, like a tiny puppy snuggled against his chest.

One Sunday something happened at the racetrack that shook up Mom and Dad to the point where even they began to think about angels. On that particular day there were footraces for the children and a micro race for the women. Then came the big event. Mom sat behind a small shaded stand next to the radio announcer but close to the track so she could keep score. All the kids were in the bleachers with Pearlie, their closest neighbor, who held Rondy. All the cars lined up, as usual. The standard formalities followed, then they were off.

Not long into the race, Rondy began crying, and Pearlie couldn't quiet him with a pacifier or toys. He wanted to nurse, and he wanted to nurse now. Pearlie paced back and forth; she bounced him, but he screamed so loud that people began complaining. Finally she sent Judy to get Mom.

Mom hurried away with Judy to the bleachers— and not a moment too soon. She had just reached the bleachers when another car hit Dad and sent him crashing into the scorekeeper's stand. He hit at such an angle that the roof of the stand caved in and boards flew through the air at a deadly speed. The radio announcer scrambled to safety, but the impact was so strong that it knocked his pants off. Ordinarily that might have been comical, but everybody knew where Mom was supposed to be. Women began screaming, and men began running to the heap of boards and rubble, expecting to pull out her mangled body.

But she wasn't there! One man even looked in the air. In the bleachers all the while, Rondy cooed and laughed to see his mama.

Had an angel pinched the baby to make him cry at just the right time? That night John read his Bible again. This time he looked in the concordance at the back. He needed to learn more about angels.

CHAPTER 7

ICY WATERS

Fall passed quickly, and soon winter blew its angry, cold breath. Snow covered the ground so deeply that all traffic temporarily halted. School was canceled, and even NASCAR called for a shutdown until warmer weather.

"John, I've made myself very clear," Mom said. "It's too cold, and you still have a touch of that flu. Stay inside!"

John's eyes narrowed. Sometimes Mom treated him as if he was a little kid. Sure, he had had the flu, and he had been throwing up. But that was yesterday, and now the whole gang was headed for Greer's Pond to ice-skate.

"You know it doesn't snow that often here in the south," John argued.

"Try to get some rest now," Mom said, ignoring his comment. "I've got tons of paperwork. If you need something, call Snookie or Judy. I don't want to be bothered."

John could hear his mother's footsteps plodding down the hallway. Then the door shut behind her. He could hear the squeak of the chair as she pulled it away from the desk. He listened. The chair squeaked again as she sat in it and scooted it closer to

36

look at her. Mom demanded to know who had thrown the offensive mud pie. Judy, Snookie, and Jimmy immediately turned and looked at John. So much for loyalty! Mom demanded that they all apologize to the woman, and as soon as she left, Mom swatted John on the leg and hissed out the familiar phrase that always sent terror to his heart: "Wait until your dad comes home!"

CHAPTER 6

ANGELS ON THE LOOKOUT

Summer was almost at an end. Dried cornstalks dotted the gardens; the tomato vines shriveled in the heat, leaving a few green pieces of fruit hiding under the parched leaves. Orange pumpkins brightened the brown fields.

Reluctantly John climbed into the blue station wagon with Judy, Jimmy, Snookie, and Mom to go shopping for school clothes. As far as he was concerned, shopping was more agonizing than going to the dentist's office. The next-worse thing was sitting in a classroom, dissecting sentences, when fish could be biting his hook as he sat under a shade tree. Or he could be spinning wheelies on his new, shiny blue bicycle.

He and Dale Earnhardt had already made up their minds that neither of them needed to finish school. Both had already learned enough to read the street signs and the directions for putting an engine together. What more did a professional race car driver need to know? Practice and determination, they reasoned, could not be found in a book.

One melodious note filled the air: the roar of engines as NASCAR prepared for the biggest races of the year. Eagerly, both boys anticipated an eventful season.

John and Dale saw each other less and less as

the desk. He could hear her shuffling papers.

Quietly he threw the covers back and tiptoed to his closet. It was so cold out that he decided he'd just leave his pajama pants on under his jeans.

Jimmy poked his head in the door. "Are you coming?"

"Yes."

His brother shrugged. "It's your funeral."

"Thanks. With a brother like you, who needs enemies?"

The two slipped to the kitchen, where Snookie banged on some pots and pans while they shut the door so Mom wouldn't hear them leave. Then the two girls followed a few minutes later.

"You're going to be in so much trouble," Judy scolded as she caught up with them. "You could catch pneumonia."

"I'm fine."

"Well, when Mom tells Dad what you've done, just leave my name out of your defense case."

"Yeah, well, who's going to test the ice if I don't come?"

They all looked at each other and shook their heads. None of them had the nerve to test the ice. Besides, John weighed the least.

"That's what I thought," John said. "You don't want to be blamed, but you want me to come."

Nobody said much as they made their way down the road.

"I heard that you can take that path by Doby's barn," Jimmy said finally, breaking the silence. "It's a straight shot to the pond."

"Let's do it," John agreed. "If Mom finds out I'm gone, she'll look first on the road."

"I'm game," Snookie said.

Within minutes they were walking through some of the thickest woods John had ever seen. The path turned out to be a deer trail that twisted and turned through briars and brambles, and one trail ran into another one. Fortunately, the sound of other boys yelling at the pond helped steer them in that direction.

It made John feel important that the gang had waited for him. "I guess I'm the only one here with an ounce of courage," he said as he stepped on the ice.

"Or the only one here without an ounce of sense," Snookie smirked.

"There's not one spot in this whole pond that is over my head," John retorted. "So even if the ice does crack I'll just get wet. At least I'm not afraid of a little water."

"Well, get on with it then," the boys yelled impatiently.

John skated cautiously, gradually working himself all around the pond. When he got to the middle, he held his thumb up. With a whoop and a yell, the others joined him on the ice. The cold air stung his face and filled his lungs. He felt great.

They skated for about two hours. Snookie and Judy kept reminding him that he needed to get back home before Mom discovered an empty bed. He'd probably be grounded, but at that point he didn't care. He rarely had a chance to slide so effortlessly over frozen water.

About noon the warmth from the sun began to

create cracks. Then John lost his balance and crashed through the ice. He laughed with everybody else as they pulled him out, dripping wet up to his waist.

"You've got to go home now," Snookie told him. "Take the shortcut through the woods."

John knew she was right. Uncontrollable shivers swept all over him.

"Hurry!" she urged him on.

John dashed off through the woods, taking the deer trail. His only thoughts now were of crawling into a hot tub of water and soaking his bones for hours. The water on his pant legs was already forming a hard crust of ice. After only a few minutes his feet felt numb and heavy.

John trudged for 20 minutes through the briars and brambles until he realized that he should have come to the road 10 minutes earlier. Obviously he had taken the wrong path. He needed to change directions—but which way? The tall trees seemed to stretch out for miles in every direction.

Doing an about-face, John took off in the opposite direction. That led him through another 20 minutes of briars and brambles. By now his head was hurting and his nose was stopped up. *OK,* he reasoned, *I'll go to the left.*

But 20 minutes later there was still nothing that looked familiar, and John felt as though he couldn't move another step. His feet had no feeling. He shouted, hoping that some of the others could hear him, but no one answered. The only thing he could hear was a dog barking in the distance.

"O God, I'm going to freeze to death!" he sobbed.

Serves you right, his conscious nagged. *Thought you were such hot stuff, didn't you? Where's the brave boy now?*

Overwhelmed with discouragement, John sank down on a log. There had to be a way out of this dilemma. It wouldn't have been such a big deal if he weren't so wet. He could have walked for hours and found something, or somebody, familiar. But every step was so painful, and he felt such a weakness coming over him. The flu. No, he wasn't over the flu. He should have listened to Mom.

OK, what does someone do when he's out of answers? John asked himself.

Then he remembered what the woman at Vacation Bible School had told him about God. He remembered the picture she had shown him of the two children on the bridge with the angel watching over them. He remembered the verses he had read in the Bible.

John felt a warm feeling sweep over him as he closed his eyes. "Lord, I know I don't deserve any help, but I'm sick, cold, and lost. Please help me out of here."

He stayed put on the log, his thoughts suddenly becoming clear. God was there. He couldn't see Him, but he felt His presence. It was warm and assuring.

If only that dog would stop barking, he thought. *That irritating bark was enough to drive any owner crazy. Why, if I had a dog like that—* Then it hit him. Where there were dogs, there were people. He'd follow the sound of the dog. It all made perfect sense now! Why hadn't he thought of it before?

With renewed energy, John set off through the woods, making just enough noise and barking sounds to keep the dog howling. The animal's yapping led him right beside Doby's barn and the road to home.

Later that afternoon as he soaked in the warmth of the tub, he thought of the warm, fuzzy feeling that he felt after praying. *God was real!* And since Mom had grounded him for three days, he'd have all weekend to think about Him.

CHAPTER 8

THE ALMOST MURDER

Eventually the snow melted. Old Man Winter sneaked out the back door of February, and March ushered in mild days. Sunshine warmed the earth, and the tiny crocus flowers popped out of the muddy ground. It was spring, John's favorite time of the year. Favorite, because he never really liked cold weather. Oh, it had its moments when snow painted the landscape white and school was canceled.

But most of the time winter wore a gray coat that left his mom depressed. With spring, though, new hope seemed to surge through her veins. She combed the nursery for new flowers to plant. Mom loved flowers. Her pink and white azaleas that lined the front of the house were the talk of the town. Yellow and white daffodils lined the pathway to the front door. Heavily scented roses of every color bloomed profusely throughout the yard, as did many other flowers that John couldn't name—nor did he care to. Flowers were pretty, but he couldn't have a decent game of tag or football without crushing one. Mom tolerated a broken mirror or muddy carpet better than she tolerated a flattened flower.

But aside from warm weather and pretty flowers, John looked forward to another birthday each spring.

Mom always made sure that everyone got something they wanted on their birthday. This year John wanted a .22 rifle so he could hunt squirrels and rabbits. Mom had promised to take him to the store and let him pick one out. The anticipation nearly drove him crazy.

March 7 dawned deliciously warm. John bounded out of bed and dressed in record speed. He found Dad in the kitchen, frying eggs. "I'm ready to go to the store!" he announced.

His dad grinned at his enthusiasm. "Stores aren't even open yet," he announced. "It's barely 7:00. What's the hurry?"

"It's my birthday!"

"So?"

"I want my rifle."

Dad shrugged. "Are you responsible enough to own a rifle?"

John rolled his eyes. "Dad, I won't shoot at any living thing other than squirrels, rabbits, and deer. I promise."

His dad remained silent as he plopped a plate of fried eggs and white rice on the table and motioned for him to sit and eat. John obeyed and poured himself a glass of orange juice. The two ate in friendly silence. The clock on the wall slowly ticked away the minutes. They had almost finished breakfast when Snookie bounded into the kitchen and sat down to eat. Ten minutes later Jimmy appeared, followed by Judy, who busied herself wiping counters and washing dishes. And so the time ticked away. Mom didn't awaken until 8:30.

"I'm ready to go!" John told her enthusiastically

as soon as she appeared in the kitchen.

His mom only grunted and poured herself a glass of milk. She looked out the window as she drank slowly, often pausing to take in the morning beauty. "I need to water my flowers first, son," she commented.

John sighed and headed outside to wait. It seemed to him that anticipation must be the hardest thing to live with. Hours later he and Mom finally drove off to pick out his rifle.

To John, it was the most beautiful gun in the world. Dad taught him how to load it and keep it properly cleaned. He spent the rest of the day in the woods shooting at targets. The gun made him feel secure, important, and powerful.

His first victim was a gray squirrel poised on a branch munching nuts. His little beady eyes were bright and watchful. This same squirrel had seen John tramping through the woods many times, and John had never attempted to harm it. Carefully John took aim and pulled the trigger. A loud bang resounded through the forest. The squirrel dropped like a leaf off the tree. Elated, John ran over and stood over his prize. Blood oozed out of the little animal's side. The bullet had gone right through the heart.

Somehow the sight of that little pile of fur, so still and motionless, caused John to hold his breath and look away. Silently he picked it up by the tail and carried it home.

Dad congratulated him on his accomplishment and showed him how to skin the little creature. Snookie cried. Judy scolded. Jimmy just looked sad. Somehow in his quest to be a man John had forgotten that Jimmy fed squirrels and built birdhouses in his spare time. Jimmy hated guns and wanted no part in killing anything.

John felt torn inside. All his friends boasted of their accuracy and skill with a gun. Some hunted wild deer with their dads. In their backwoods neighborhood killing animals was an accepted part of life. It was something people had done for centuries in order to survive. After skinning the squirrel, he had no desire to hunt again.

Not long after that a one-armed man began coming around the house when Dad was away on trips. It seemed to John that Mom glowed in the man's presence.

One warm August afternoon John rounded the corner of the house and saw his mom and the man standing beside the man's car, talking and laughing. Then the man reached over and touched Mom's cheek. He was smiling. John wanted to wipe that man's smile right off his face. It looked to him like this man was stealing Mom from his dad. And since Dad wasn't there, it was up to John to take care of the situation.

Angry, John crept back around the corner and headed for the back door. He dashed through the house and grabbed his .22 rifle. (He'd been itching to use it on something other than squirrels.) This lowlife had no right to break up families. He was scum! Didn't he know that Mom had five kids?

He loaded his gun, opened the bedroom window, cocked it, and took careful aim at the man's head. His index finger felt for the trigger. *Steady now,* he told himself. *Hold it steady.*

"Just do it!" the evil angels must have whispered. "Pull the trigger!"

John had no idea what made him hesitate. Maybe in the back of his head he was remembering what death looked like on a squirrel. Human life was a gift from God. Did he—or anyone else—have the right to take it away?

If only he'd had heavenly vision, he could have seen an intense battle between the good angels and the evil ones. In that moment both were battling for his soul. As the tears streamed down his cheeks, he watched the man get into his car and drive away.

A few months after that experience Dad announced that they were moving to Florida. John wondered if Dad was trying to keep the family together and get Mom away from the one-armed man. Did Dad really think he could make more money building highways? Or were the folks convinced that a racetrack wasn't the best influence on the kids? John never knew for sure. All he knew was that his world was crashing down around him. Nothing would ever be the same again.

Buddy's Gang

can't believe it!" John shouted. "You're closing the track, and we're moving *where?*"

"Calm down, son," James Earnhardt said quietly. "This is for your own good."

"*My* good! How is jerking me out of school and moving me halfway across the country for my good?"

"We are not 'jerking' you out of school," Mom told him. "Your dad and I feel that it would be best to get you kids into another environment. He's found a steady job that will pay good money. Business at the Grill has slowed down, and so has the track. NASCAR has taken over the Sunday racing business."

"Don't worry"—Snookie put her arm around John's shoulder—"Florida is a great place to live. There are alligators and year-round sunshine."

"Better schools, too," Jimmy added.

John shook his head as he stalked out the front door. "Crazy!" he yelled back. "This is crazy!"

"Johnny, come back here!" his mother commanded.

"Let him go," he heard his father say. "He'll be fine once we get there."

With a heavy heart he wandered down to the vacant racetrack. The stands were empty, but in his mind he could see the wheels spinning, the crowds cheering, the dust swirling. He could smell the pop-corn and feel the gentle sun on his shoulders. He could see the places where he and the other boys his age played marbles or spun around on their bikes while waiting for the races to begin.

Maybe all his friends would forget him. It just wasn't fair! How could he leave all this? Saying good-bye was bad enough, but being the new kid at school would be worse. All new kids were snubbed at school. *He* wasn't even kind to new kids when they came to his school. Now he would know what it felt like.

It didn't take long for Mom to find renters for the house. At least his parents had promised they wouldn't sell it, that one day they'd move back. Maybe he'd be old enough then to reopen the track and compete himself.

Dad tried to lift John's spirits by promising to take him to the races on Daytona Beach. "You'll see real racing there, son," he said. "No doubt Ralph and Dale will show up sometime."

The day came when the last box was packed and the last goodbye said. Grandma and Grandpa Earnhardt came to see them off. Grandpa seemed worried about something other than the move. John could hear him speaking in low tones to his parents. He circled around and hid behind a nearby tree.

"It was bad enough for your sister to join that strange church and run off to their college in Tennessee," Grandpa told Dad. "But now she's moved out to California to another one of their schools. I think she's been brainwashed."

Dad nodded in agreement. "Craziest thing I ever heard of, keeping Saturday for Sunday."

"At least she keeps one day holy," Grandma said grimly, looking straight at Dad. Grandma always made it known that she didn't approve of Dad keeping the racetrack open on Sundays.

"Are you trying to tell me that racing isn't a holy activity?" Dad joked.

John walked away, now sure that they weren't going to talk about anything interesting. He vaguely knew his aunt Jeanette. She usually visited once during the summer, and sometimes at Christmas. She always smiled a lot and gave books for presents. John thought books made strange Christmas presents. He shook his head. Now wasn't the time to be thinking of his aunt and her religious beliefs. He had problems enough of his own.

Mom yelled for him to kiss Grandma goodbye. The old woman's eyes brimmed with tears. "You be good, and read that Bible I gave you," she said to John.

John nodded, and then they were off.

: : : : : :

It didn't take the family long to get settled into their new home. It took longer to feel "settled" when it came to school. Had it not been for Snookie and Jimmy, John would have run away. There was just something comforting about knowing someone else in that new place, even if it was your older siblings.

Every day after school he rode his bike around town. There were neat springs to swim in and lots of hard-packed trails for riding. John's real intention was to be where the other boys were, so they would notice him.

"Hey, you!" one of them finally yelled. "Wanna ride with us?"

John tried to be cool, so he just shrugged. "Depends on where you're riding."

"Down to the drugstore," the biggest boy answered. "Old man Stubbs is real good about giving us free stuff."

"Really?" John perked up. "What kind of stuff?"

"Water guns, candy, all kinds of stuff."

"Let's go!"

John yanked back on his handlebars, making his bike stand up on the back wheel.

The four boys pedaled down the back streets, then cut across to Main. The leader of the pack was a tanned boy named Buddy. He was tall and slender with a wide grin that lit up his face. John immediately liked him.

He followed as, one by one, the boys parked their bikes in the alley beside the brick drugstore. "Just watch us and do what we do," Buddy instructed him.

They casually walked into the store and meandered down the aisles. As they passed the gum, Buddy picked up a pack. "You like the pink kind, John?"

"Yeah, it's good."

Buddy slipped it into John's pocket and winked. "Personally," he whispered, "I like the grape." He picked up a pack and bent down, appearing to tie his shoe. But when he straightened up, the gum was gone. He did the same thing with the water guns.

One went in his pocket, and he stuck another one in his shoe.

John wondered how he managed to walk. He was too confused to know what to do. If he didn't go along with them, they would snub him even more at school. But if he got caught shoplifting, he'd have to face the police and his parents. He just followed the other boys in a daze.

After a few minutes they all turned and headed for the door, walking out as casually as they had walked in.

Suddenly two strong arms grabbed John and Buddy by the shoulder. "What do you boys think you're doing?" a deep voice demanded.

John stared up at a tall, thin man whose big hands easily gripped his and Buddy's shoulders so firmly the boys could barely move.

"What are you boys doing?" the man repeated sternly.

John gulped and began stammering, but Buddy remained cool. "Nothing, Mr. Stubbs. We're just looking around."

"We both know better than that," the man replied. "Don't you boys know that shoplifting is stealing? I couldn't afford to stay in business if I let you come in and take anything you wanted. I would have to raise my prices on everything just to pay for what you take. That makes other people have to pay more."

"What's wrong, Lewis?" a woman from behind the counter asked.

"I caught a gang of shoplifters. Phone the police!"

The police! John felt the color draining from his

face. What would the police do to them? What would his parents do when they found out?

"Oh, please, sir!" Buddy cried out. "My father will kill me."

"You should have thought of that sooner," the pharmacist replied.

"Please have mercy!" John suddenly blurted out. "We'll give everything back and never steal anything again."

"Mercy," the man repeated softly, as if to himself. "Now, what would you know about mercy?" He gazed earnestly into John's eyes.

"If you'll forgive me, I'll not only give them back, but I'll promise never to step foot in here again."

"Is that so?"

"I promise."

Mr. Stubbs' hand relaxed on their shoulders. John pulled the gum and everything else he had stolen out of his pockets and handed it to the pharmacist. Reluctantly the others did the same. Buddy handed him a water gun and a small pocketknife that John hadn't even seen him take. How in the world had he gotten all that stuff without him seeing it? And he had been right behind him!

"OK, boys," Mr. Stubbs said. "I don't want to see you in this store without your parents. Is that clear?"

The whole group nodded and began bumping into each other in their haste to get out before Mr. Stubbs changed his mind.

When they reached the alley, Buddy bent over and ceremoniously pulled out a second water gun that was wedged between his sock and high-top shoe.

"That's why you always take two," he gloated.

The others gave him a high five. "Good going, Buddy!" they shouted.

John stood there in disbelief. Mr. Stubbs had been so kind to them. It just didn't seem right. "I gotta go," he finally said as he mounted his bike.

"See you tomorrow," the others called to him as they rode off.

John didn't reply. Those boys were considered cool by most of the kids at school. Yet they boldly lied and stole from a man who had just showed mercy to them. *At least I won't ever steal from him again,* he reasoned.

It wasn't long, though, until John pushed the still small voice of conscience aside and continued to hang out with Buddy and his gang.

■ ■ ■ ■ ■ ■

The years passed, and now Dad was ready to move back to North Carolina. All during the time they lived in Florida they had kept track of Ralph Earnhardt and his son Dale. Both boys had changed so much.

John came back to North Carolina riding a red motorcycle, even though he was only 15 years old. (At that time the state of Florida allowed a teen to get a driver's license at the age of 14.) But once he arrived in North Carolina a state trooper pulled him over and forced him to park it.

Since he couldn't ride his motorcycle on the state highway, John often went down to the decaying race-track and spun around the curves. Sometimes he stopped and thought about all the fun he and Dale had had while watching the cars zoom past the checkered flag. Two boys with big dreams of one day living a life of speed and glory. Somehow the dream had lost its intensity for John.

Dad now scoffed at the idea of reopening the track. Micro-midget racing was not big enough to compete with NASCAR. Racing was slowly becoming a full-time sport, not a part-time pleasure.

Dale, however, had remained steadfast in his quest to be with his dad on the track. He thought of little else besides racing. He wasn't happy going to school. He and his dad fought over it constantly.

"It was the only thing I ever let my daddy down over," Dale would say later. "He wanted me to finish. It was the only thing he ever pleaded with me to do. But I was so hardheaded. For about a year and a half after that, we didn't have a close relationship."

Ralph Earnhardt was a master mechanic and began teaching Dale how to build engines. Sometimes he'd give Dale used tires and various car parts to tinker with. As soon as he received his license, Dale began speeding through life in the fast lane, driving any vehicle he could scrape up the money for.

As for John, he knew his life would take a different direction, but he didn't know where.

CHAPTER 10

THE LICENSE

Eventually the day arrived when John turned 16 and was able to take the test and apply for a driver's license. Later that night he cradled the small card in his hand. Now he could drive in whichever state he chose! He stared at his picture. Mom said he should have smiled bigger—but that would have looked like he was overeager. Nah! Only nerds smiled real big for their driver's license picture.

"Let me see it," his dad said, leaning over the chair where John sat in the warm sunny kitchen. John handed him the license. His father held it out from his face in an effort to see better. "H'mmm, I can't see your eyes."

"Daaaad!" John reached for the license. "You need glasses."

His dad turned slightly, holding John at bay. "Really. I can't see your eyes! How can they use this picture to identify you? Boy, you need a haircut. Are you that broke? What does a cut cost now, $5?

John groaned. Not again! Why did everybody have to make such a big deal over the length of his hair? He heard it in every class at school. He heard it when he walked by the principal standing in the hall. He had studied about the price Americans paid to have freedom. He knew that in the old days men wore wigs made of long hair. Even George Washington, the first president of the United States, wore a long braid down his back. What was the big deal over a little hair touching your eyebrows or your ears?

He winced. Perhaps changing the subject would get Dad talking about something else. "Dad, I want to go look at cars this week."

"You got any money?"

"Some."

"How much is 'some'?"

John shrugged. "A couple hundred."

His dad took a deep breath. "That's not enough to buy a good car." He looked at John's crestfallen face. "But maybe we can look anyway. I've got a load to deliver in my truck tomorrow. How about Friday?"

John perked up. "You mean it?"

"Yeah, we'll look. Are you sure you can see to drive?"

It was past 7:00 on Friday evening when Dad walked in the door, tired, hungry, and dirty. John wasn't in the mood to hear his excuses. Hadn't his dad made a promise? *Why,* he wondered, *were parents so irresponsible? Especially when it came to things that were important to their children.* He had been pacing the floor since 4:00 that afternoon.

"What kind of car are you looking for?" his weary dad asked as they climbed into his truck and headed for the used car lot.

John braced himself for his Dad's reaction. "I'd like a 1955 Chevy."

"I can't believe you!" his father sputtered.

"We've always had Fords in this family. Why would you want a Chevy?"

"I like 'em."

"You trying to make me the laughing stock of the family? I can just hear Ralph and Dale going on about that."

"They'd drive anything that ran."

"Ralph races in a Ford all the time—and wins!" his dad reminded him.

They drove the rest of the way to the used car lot in silence. Neither said much as they surveyed the lot. His dad stopped to admire a black Ford Starliner. Next to that was a 1964 Ford Falcon. John briefly noticed the sky-blue color, the chrome wheels, and the modified engine with a stick shift in the floor.

Then he saw it—a 1955 Chevy sitting in the corner like a lovely pearl in the midst of sewage. It was love at first sight. He raced over and gingerly touched the dark metallic-blue hood. He gently lifted it and gaped at the souped-up 283 engine. Closing it carefully, he walked around the body, taking in the mag wheels and the dent-free sides. The doors were locked, but he could see the four-speed stick shift on the floor. This was it—the car of his dreams!

Of course it took some work to convince Dad that it was a good car. After a few days of constant begging, pleading, and pledging to work for the rest of his life, John proudly drove the blue Chevy home.

The car did little to increase John's attentiveness at school. He stayed out late each night with his friends and dozed during class the next day. He sped through town on his first date in the blue Chevy (now lovingly called "Betsy"), and received his first ticket.

His teachers tried to impress him with the importance of an education but, like Dale, John had already made up his mind that education was a pain in the neck.

While hanging out with Buddy and his gang in Florida, John had begun smoking cigarettes. As he got older it became a three-pack-a-day habit. The school principal dismissed him from school in the tenth grade for smoking in the school bathroom. Unable to find a good job, he went to work on the second shift at Cannon Mills, where Dale Earnhardt was working. Except that Dale was working on the first shift. John actually passed Dale each day as he came in to work. Like John, Dale wasn't real happy working in a textile mill, and went through several different jobs. None of them lasted for long—his heart was in stock car racing. He didn't want to do anything but be out on that track with his dad, Ralph Earnhardt.

It was discouraging at first, but somehow Dale worked and scraped until he was able to compete in a Sportsman race with his father. Of course, Dale didn't have the experience the other drivers had. One veteran driver simply wouldn't let him go by. Dale did everything he knew to do to pass, but couldn't. His car simply didn't have the power. His father, who was already a lap ahead, came up from behind and put his bumper against Dale's. He pushed him right by the other racer, enabling Dale to win third place.

In many ways God is like that. He is our heavenly Father who is ready to do whatever He can to help us in our difficulties. We can't defeat the devil by our own power, but if we give Him the steering wheel of our life and ask Him to do what we can't, He will steer us through the bad times and across the finish line.

The Bible says that God is like a shepherd caring for his sheep. "He shall feed his flock like a shepherd: he shall gather the lambs with his arm, and carry them in his bosom" (Isaiah 40:11).

CHAPTER II

A Tale of Death and Life

One evening John came home from work to find his mom in tears. Her sister had been killed in a car accident.

Not long after that mournful time a tall, gray-haired woman knocked on the door and explained that her church had heard of the death in the family. She said she had come to offer prayer and comfort and asked if we would be interested in learning about what happens after death.

John's mom agreed, and the woman, Grace Robbins, began coming to their home every week to give Bible studies. It was through that series of studies that John heard a Bible verse that changed his life forever: "Do you not know that your body is a temple of the Holy Spirit, who is in you, whom you have received from God? You are not your own; you were bought at a price. Therefore honor God with your body" (1 Corinthians 6:19, 20, NIV).

It was as though God had taken him by the shoulder and said, "John, I want to be with you always. I want to live in you. Invite Me into your heart, John. I died so that we could always be together."

Understanding dawned in his mind gradually, like the morning sun gliding over the hills and valleys.

Our bodies don't belong to us anymore. They are supposed to be the dwelling place for the Holy Spirit. "For ye are bought with a price," the Bible says, "therefore glorify God in your body." The price that the Bible refers to is the blood of Jesus. The purpose of His death was to pay for our sins, because we could not pay for them. The reward of accepting Jesus was to have Him dwell in us and offer us the promise of a resurrection morning when all the righteous dead are raised to life eternal (1 Thessalonians 4:16).

More than anything John wanted Jesus to dwell in him. He went outside that night. The heavens were bright, and the night air felt cool. As he looked up in the star-studded sky, he realized he wasn't alone. God was there. He could feel a divine presence as close to him as the cigarettes in his shirt pocket.

"All right, God," he declared as he fell down on his knees, "You win. I give myself to You." He took the cigarettes out of his pocket and crushed them in the dirt. "Please take these evils away from me. In the name of Jesus, I claim the victory over them. Live in this temple as You have promised."

A peace washed over him. He quietly went inside and crawled into bed. From that moment on John Earnhardt had a new purpose in life. He began studying the Bible with a passion. He discovered that God wanted to be with His people so much that He set aside a special day, called the Sabbath, so they could be together.

It all began to make sense. He remembered when Aunt Jeanette had begun keeping Saturday instead of Sunday. She said the Ten Commandments, written by God's finger, specifically called the seventh day of the week the Sabbath day (Exodus 20:8-11). The whole family thought she'd been brainwashed. John discovered that his Aunt Jeanette wasn't crazy after all—now they all thought that *he* was the wacky one!

"You're crazy!" his friends told him. "There are so many things Christians can't do. We're going to save religion for when we get old. *Then* we'll become Christians."

"I want to give God the very best of my life," John told them. He was glad he did. As the years passed, he watched as those same friends went through some terrible times. One of them suffered two broken marriages, and another one was killed while he was driving under the influence of drugs. If only they had invited Jesus to live in their heart their lives would have been so much happier!

Meanwhile, John was praying that God would show him what he should do as a lifework. At that time he was building caskets at a casket company. He certainly didn't want to spend the rest of his life doing that. He no longer felt the desire to race like his father had. So he prayed, and Jesus answered his prayer.

At night John began having strange dreams. In his dreams he was always standing before a group of people, holding an open Bible in his hand. It became clear to him that he was being called to the ministry. Instead of building caskets for the dead, he would be an instrument to bring people to life, spiritually speaking.

He began selling Christian books. But after three years John didn't see his prospects of becoming a minister any closer to realization. He could barely pay his bills. He asked his parents to help pay the expenses of going to a Christian college, but it didn't work out.

"God," John prayed, "if You will provide the funds for the first year of college, I will know that this is what You want me to do."

He went on the scholarship plan in which the local church conference would hold his salary for a summer. Then at the end of the summer the conference, the book company, and the college would add a percentage to what he had sold.

As soon as John went on the scholarship program, his sales tripled! At the end of the summer he had enough to pay for the first year of college. There was no doubt in his mind that God had called him to be a minister.

∎ ∎ ∎ ∎ ∎ ∎

Meanwhile, 15 miles away, young Dale Earnhardt was going through a battle of his own. On September 26, 1973, Dale's father died of a heart attack while he was rebuilding a carburetor in his backyard garage. The family buried him in a small Kannapolis cemetery with a car on his tombstone.

And that was the legacy Ralph left for Dale: racing. His mother gave him the two cars in the garage that his father had competed in. It was a sad event, but it proved to be the turning point in Dale's career. He said later, "I'd give up everything I have if he were still alive, but I don't think I'd be where I am if he hadn't died."

Dale had two cars and was now ready to show the

world that he was indeed the son of Ralph Earnhardt. He would be a winner, but it would take work and precision driving. In field workouts he practiced pin-point accuracy by plucking ivy off a wall every time he drove by.

Dale raced on weekends, but during the week he toiled as a welder and mechanic. He struggled for five years, borrowing money during the week to buy groceries for his family, hoping to win it back in a race over the weekend. He later described himself as "wild and crazy, young and dumb."

Dale Earnhardt may have been a man of few words, but during a race he took chances that no others even dreamed of. He carefully planned his every move, often hanging back until the last couple of laps.

While Dale was learning how to win a race, John was learning how to win people to God's kingdom. Their roads were now going in different directions.

CHAPTER 12

JOHN MEETS MR. STUBBS AND THE ONE-ARMED MAN

Through the years John served the Lord in various positions. Once he served as a pastor for seven years in South Carolina. Imagine his surprise when one of his church members, an older retired man, told him that he and his wife used to live in Florida and owned a drugstore.

John tried to remember the name of the pharmacist from whom he had stolen candy and water guns when he hung out with Buddy and his gang. It had been so long ago. . . He couldn't remember his name, but he did remember the name of the town.

"Was your drugstore in Forrest City?" he asked.

"How did you know?" the older man asked, surprised.

John told his story about being caught shoplifting.

Mr. Stubbs laughed. "It was probably me," he said. "I caught more than one boy shoplifting in my store."

John often wondered what happened to Buddy. He had heard that Buddy was in prison, and he didn't doubt the story. Small crimes usually turn into bigger ones. A little candy today, and a water gun tomorrow, then a pocketknife, each item more expensive than the last. The thrill of outsmarting the clerks would soon become addictive, like smoking cigarettes or using drugs.

He often wondered what his life would have been like had he followed Buddy and his gang much longer. Maybe he too would be in prison. Or what if he had decided to be a race car driver like Dale Earnhardt? Would he have been happy? Dale certainly seemed to be. He liked nothing better than the thrill of racing and driving past that checkered flag. Yet somehow John knew he wouldn't have been that happy.

He remembered holding a series of evangelistic meetings in Ohio. A woman attended who was always dressed fashionably. From appearances, she seemed to have everything the world could offer. But John read in her eyes a different story. She wasn't happy. She wasn't satisfied with material things. About halfway through the meetings, she confessed that she stopped by the bar on her way home from work each evening—and on the way home from the meetings each night.

As the meetings progressed, John was able to give this woman a clear picture of God and His love for her. The next night she didn't stop at the bar on the way home from work. Gradually she was able to stop going to the bar after the meetings. Her whole life changed, and her face showed the difference. There was a light in her eyes that had not been there before. It gave John great satisfaction in knowing that he'd had a small part in giving her hope and happiness.

Not long after that he was browsing through a sporting store. He really hadn't planned to go into this particular store, but as he was driving by he just felt the urge to stop. He browsed for a few minutes, taking time to examine the rows of fishing gear and camping equipment. He was about ready to leave when a male voice asked, "Let me know if I can help you find something."

When John looked up, there was the same one-armed man he'd almost shot when he was a child. Of course, the man didn't recognize him and wouldn't have known that John had once stood in the window with a gun aimed at his head while he was talking with John's mother.

"I'm John Earnhardt," John introduced himself. "You many not remember me, but I remember seeing you at our house many years ago. My parents are Julia and James Earnhardt.

The man acted surprised and almost embarrassed. The two men chatted for a few minutes. John was about to leave when the man extended his one good arm and touched John. "I just want you to know that I'm a Christian now," he said. "God has changed my life."

"And to think," John told his wife later, "I almost killed that man because he was trying to break up my family. He would have died in his sins, never knowing Jesus. I know now why God wrote in the Ten Commandments, 'Thou shalt not kill.' God is the only judge who can read hearts."

CHAPTER 13

THE FINAL RACE

Dear Dale,

It's been a long time since we played around my father's racetrack in Gold Hill. Our paths have surely gone in different directions! You are doing exactly what you've always wanted to do. Congratulations on your recent wins!

I want to share with you what has happened in my life. Just a few years ago I became a Christian. Words can't express what a difference Jesus Christ has made in my life and in my marriage. I don't know what your relationship with the Lord is, but I can testify that He has made a difference in this Carolina boy. I am enclosing some material that I've found helpful.

John

: : : : : :

Staring at the envelope in his hand, John prayed that it would touch Dale's life, and then dropped it in the outgoing mail. Four hundred miles separated them.

All afternoon John thought about Dale, who had won championship after championship, making more money in one year than John hoped to see in a lifetime.

A few weeks later John received an envelope from Dale. He had sent an autographed picture of himself standing in front of his car with a short note: "John, thanks for the letter. Dale."

∷ ∷ ∷

May 30, 1993

It was one of those rare occasions when John and his dad were able to sit down and watch a race together. It was the Coca-Cola 600, held on Memorial Day weekend. Dale had been in front for 64 laps, fending off challenges from top drivers, such as Ernie Irvan, Rusty Wallace, and Dale Jarrett, when he pitted after 220 laps and was penalized for speeding in pit row. Determined to catch up, Dale tried to get around Greg Sacks. Suddenly, Greg spun sideways, and the sportscaster began shouting that Dale had tagged Greg. Dale was penalized one lap for rough driving.

John and his dad sighed. Put back a whole lap! There was little chance that Dale could catch up. Plainly infuriated, Dale was even more determined to show the world what he was made of. He put the pedal to the metal, and minutes later the sportscasters were shouting again.

"What a battle for the lead! Earnhardt and Ernie Irvan are wheel to wheel! And Earnhardt goes back in front!"

John sat back in the recliner and watched Dale fly by the checkered flag, savoring his third 600 win and his fifty-fifth victory. His determination to fight against the odds made the ride in victory lane even sweeter.

∎ ∎ ∎ ∎ ∎ ∎

Dear Dale,

I'm going to be in your area conducting a seminar on the book of Revelation next month. I would love to see you. Can you come?

John

No reply. John knelt in prayer. Please, God, touch his life. Help him to see his need of You.

∎ ∎ ∎ ∎ ∎ ∎

The years continued to roll by. John, now married and with two children, traveled around the world with the Amazing Facts Radio and TV Ministry, spreading the news that Jesus is soon coming. While they were in the Philippines baptizing 1,000 people from a series of meetings, Dale was enjoying his title as "The Intimidator."

Once back in the States, John heard that Dale was signing autographs in the High Point, North Carolina, mall. He walked in just as Dale looked up from signing a T-shirt. There were about 300 people waiting in line to see him.

Dale smiled and waved.

John waited a few minutes. Suddenly Dale looked at his watch. John hurried over just as two men from NASCAR were whisking him away from the crowd. Dale paused and waited for John to catch up.

"Dale," John exclaimed. "It's so good to see you."

"Hello, John Earnhardt," Dale smiled. "Good to see you, too." He looked tired.

The two men with him moved about impatiently. "Dale, we're going to get mobbed here in a few minutes," one of them warned.

When a crowd of people began moving toward them, the men grabbed Dale's arm and pulled him away. Dale's fame had cost him his privacy.

Not long after seeing Dale in the mall, John met Lois Tyler. Her husband, Carl, had been a professional race car driver in NASCAR's beginning. He had given his heart to the Lord and had been baptized after learning about the Sabbath. Although he had died some years before, Lois continued to go to the races and witness to the drivers.

One week she said to Dale, "It's OK to be known as The Intimidator when you're behind the wheel. But you need to be nicer to people."

Dale smiled at her. "Lois, would you like to go with me to victory lane?"

Lois would later say, "Dale made a real effort to reach out to people after that day. Stories began to leak out about him visiting children in the hospital, and giving money to pay for a church parking lot."

Together, Lois and John began to plan how they could get a Bible course into the hands of the drivers and race car fans. John and his wife wrote a little pamphlet that compared a car race to the spiritual race we all must run (1 Corinthians. 9:24, 25). Lois included it in the thousands of packets of literature she gave out each week.

On February 18, 2001, John and his wife, Crystal, were conducting evangelistic meetings in North Carolina, where John now worked as an evangelist.

On that Sunday afternoon they sat in front of the TV, watching the race in Daytona, Florida.

As usual, there were several wrecks. One driver tapped another driver from behind, spinning him into another driver. That driver was sent tumbling through the air, flipping twice. Everyone held their breath as the driver walked away from his car.

On the last lap the crowd became ecstatic. Waltrip, who drove one of Dale's cars, was in the lead, and Dale's son was in second place. It seemed as though Dale, in third place, had decided to protect the two drivers in front of him by preventing anyone else from passing.

Suddenly Dale's car wiggled slightly. Then it veered left, took an abrupt right, and got hit on the passenger side by Ken Schrader before barreling nearly head-on into the wall. Waltrip cruised down victory lane while Dale Junior jumped out of his car and dashed to his father's side. No one suspected more than a few scratches to be on Dale—he had walked away from worse wrecks than this.

With the race over, another program came on. It was time to leave for the meetings, so John turned off the TV.

Five minutes before he stood up to preach, a man rushed into the meeting hall and handed John an announcement that Dale had died from a severe injury to his head. Stunned, John spent a few minutes talking about Dale and asked the audience to pray with him. It was the first time he had ever had difficulty focusing on a sermon. Even so, some said it was one of the finest messages they'd heard on God's love.

Later, Lois told John that one of the drivers' wives always put a Bible verse in each car before a race. Somehow, with the race about to begin, Dale hadn't received his verse. He refused to start the race that day until he had been given his Bible verse. His verse read, "The name of the Lord is a strong tower: the righteous runneth into it, and is safe" (Proverbs 18:10).

Sometimes people ask John to talk about Dale. This is what he says:

"I'd rather talk about the big race. How do we win? There is only one way: Jesus must be in control of the wheel. This is the secret to the Christian's flight to victory lane. We are to live for Christ with as much passion and intensity as Dale Earnhardt put into his racing. He never gave up. He lived each day, preparing for a race and focusing on that finish line.

"God does not care if we come in first or last. He just wants us to finish the race and cross over to victory lane, where Jesus is waiting with arms open wide."